My Canada
QUÉBEC

By Sheila Yazdani

TABLE OF CONTENTS

Québec 3

Glossary 22

Index 24

A Crabtree Seedlings Book

Crabtree Publishing
crabtreebooks.com

School-to-Home Support for Caregivers and Teachers

This book helps children grow by letting them practice reading. Here are a few guiding questions to help the reader build his or her comprehension skills. Possible answers appear in red.

Before Reading:

- What do I know about Québec?
    - *I know that Québec is a province.*
    - *I know that French is the official language of Québec.*

- What do I want to learn about Québec?
    - *I want to learn which famous people were born in Québec.*
    - *I want to learn what the provincial flag looks like.*

During Reading:

- What have I learned so far?
    - *I have learned that Québec City is the capital of Québec.*
    - *I have learned that Québec City was founded by Samuel de Champlain in 1608.*

- I wonder why...
    - *I wonder why the provincial flower is the blue flag iris.*
    - *I wonder why Québec grows so many blueberries.*

After Reading:

- What did I learn about Québec?
    - *I have learned that you can ski at Mont-Tremblant.*
    - *I have learned that the provincial bird is the snowy owl.*

- Read the book again and look for the glossary words.
    - *I see the word **capital** on page 6, and the word **fjord** on page 16. The other glossary words are found on pages 22 and 23.*

I live in Gatineau. My city is near the Ottawa River.

I can see **Parliament** Hill across the river!

Québec is a **province** in northeastern Canada. The **capital** is Québec City.

Fun Fact: Montréal is the largest city in Québec.

The provincial bird is the snowy owl.

Fun Fact: Québec grows more than 54 million kilograms (120 million pounds) of blueberries a year.

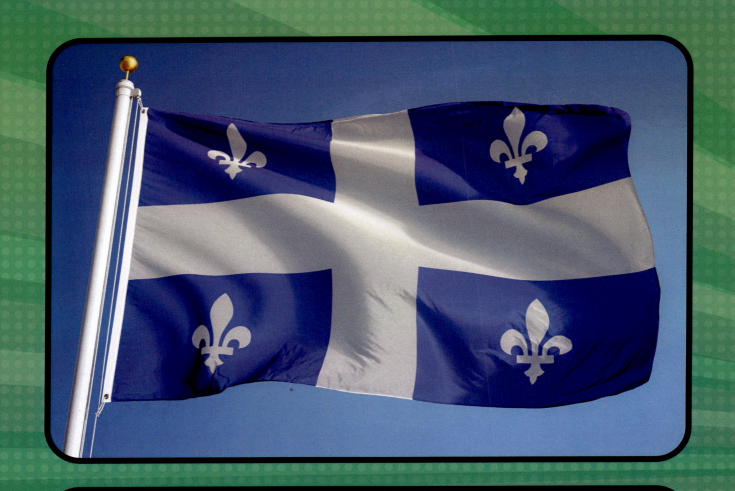

My provincial flag is blue with a white cross. It has four **fleurs-de-lis**.

My family likes to watch CF Montréal play soccer.

Fun Fact: Québec City was **founded** by Samuel de Champlain in 1608.

Sometimes I can see whales at Saguenay **Fjord**.

My family has fun skating at the Old Port of Montréal.

Actor Yanic Truesdale was born in Québec. Mixed martial arts fighter Georges St-Pierre was also born in Québec.

Fun Fact: Pierre Trudeau, former prime minister of Canada, was born in Montréal, Québec.

I enjoy seeing snow leopards at Zoo de Granby.

Glossary

capital (CAP-ih-tuhl): The city or town where the government of a country, state, or province is located

fjord (fyord): A long and narrow body of water with steep sides or cliffs

fleurs-de-lis (fler-deh-LEE): Symbols that resemble a lily flower

founded (FOUN-ded): Created or set up

parliament (PAR-luh-muhnt): The group of people who make the laws for a country

province (PROV-ins): One of the large areas that some countries, such as Canada, are divided into

Index

blueberries 10, 11
Ottawa River 4, 5
Petit-Champlain 14
Québec City 6, 14, 15
skiing 21
Truesdale, Yanic 18

About the Author

Sheila Yazdani lives in Ontario near Niagara Falls with her dog Daisy. She likes to travel across Canada to learn about its history, people, and landscape. She loves to cook new dishes she learns about. Her favorite treat is Nanaimo bars.

Written by: Sheila Yazdani
Designed and Illustrated by: Bobbie Houser
Series Development: James Earley
Proofreader: Melissa Boyce
Educational Consultant: Marie Lemke M.Ed.

Photographs:
Alamy: IanDagnall Computing: p. 15, 23; Tim Graham: p. 19
Shutterstock: Diego Grandi: cover; JHVEPhoto: p. 3; Henryk Sadura: p. 4; Facto Photo: p. 5, 23; Media Guru: p. 6, 22-23; f11photo: p. 7; Jim Cumming: p. 8; wjarek: p. 9; Bryan Pollard: p. 10-11; Krasula: p. 11; railway fx: p. 12, 22; lev radin: p. 13; Kristi Blokhin: p. 14-15; M. Etcheverry: p. 16, 22; meunierd: p. 17; DFree: p. 18 left; Featureflash Photo Agency: p. 18 right; Anne Richard: p. 20; Vlad G: p. 21

Crabtree Publishing

crabtreebooks.com   800-387-7650
Copyright © 2025 Crabtree Publishing
All rights reserved. No part of this publication may be reproduced, stored in a retrieval system or be transmitted in any form or by any means, electronic, mechanical, photocopying, recording, or otherwise, without the prior written permission of Crabtree Publishing. In Canada: We acknowledge the financial support of the Government of Canada through the Canada Book Fund for our publishing activities.

Printed in Canada/012024/CP20231127

Published in Canada
Crabtree Publishing
616 Welland Avenue
St. Catharines, Ontario
L2M 5V6

Published in the United States
Crabtree Publishing
347 Fifth Avenue
Suite 1402-145
New York, New York, 10016

Library and Archives Canada Cataloguing in Publication
Available at Library and Archives Canada

Library of Congress Cataloging-in-Publication Data
Available at the Library of Congress

Hardcover: 978-1-0398-3856-7
Paperback: 978-1-0398-3941-0
Ebook (pdf): 978-1-0398-4022-5
Epub: 978-1-0398-4094-2